Made in the USA
Monee, IL
13 October 2022

15793581R00063